# GOD KNOWS ABOUT JOY

MW00628010

## Biblical Reflections
## To Lift Up The Heart

The Fun Nun®
Sister Mary Christelle Macaluso, RSM, OFN, PhD

web site: http://www.speakers-podium.com/funnun
FUN NUN® BOOKS
COLLEGE OF SAINT MARY
OMAHA, NEBRASKA USA 68124-2377

Layout by Shirley Trout
Cover Design by Carol Sayers
Printed in the United States of America by Paragon Printing, Omaha, Nebraska

15 14 13 12 11 10 9 8 7 6 5 4 3 2 1

Copyright© 1998 by The Fun Nun®, Sister M. Christelle Macaluso, RSM, OFN, PhD
Library of Congress Catalog Card Number: 98-96129
ISBN: 0-9663462-0-3

Publisher:     Fun Nun® Books
                    College of Saint Mary
                    Omaha, Nebraska USA 68124-2377
                    Phone: 402-399-2474  FAX: 402-399-2686
                    Email: funnun@csm.edu
                    Web Site: http://www.speakers-podium.com/funnun

# DEDICATION

*To all those who are living their lives with heavy hearts.*

*To all those who are living their lives with joyful hearts.*

*To all those who are looking for a deeper meaning in life.*

*To all those who are looking for God.*

*To all those who have found God.*

# ACKNOWLEDGMENTS

No book ever comes to completion without the involvement of many people. Surely this book is no exception. I am grateful to Carol Corey. From the very first day she shared my vision, encouraged me, and worked endlessly along the way. I'm indebted to Shirley Trout, author of *Light Dances* (1997), who shared her gifts with me in so many ways — especially her insights and her professional knowledge about writing books. I also want to thank her for the lovely layout of the book. I am grateful to Mark Darby who published his first book, *Use It or Lose It*, in 1997 and who shared with me valuable information on book publication. I am grateful to Kathy Larsen for the publication of her first book *77 Secrets to Leadership Success* in 1997, which inspired me (unknown to her!) to publish my own. I have my dear friend, Marcia Borello, to thank for the title of this book, and the Sisters of Mercy who have always encouraged my endeavors. I appreciate the College of Saint Mary for all its support, and Polly Nimmer, Evelyn Whitehill and Sr. Renee Mirkes, OSF, for their editorial advice. Thanks to my family and friends who supported my goals and to any of you I may have forgotten.

# ABOUT THE AUTHOR

The Fun Nun®, Sister Mary Christelle Macaluso, RSM, OFN, PhD, has been a full-time professional speaker since 1980. She speaks nationally and internationally to business, health, education, government, religious and social groups. The Fun Nun® has been on many radio talk shows and has appeared on national television. She is a member of the National Speakers Association.

Before becoming a professional speaker, The Fun Nun® taught for 16 years at the College of Saint Mary in Omaha, Nebraska. Her educational background includes a BS from the College of Saint Mary, a MS from the University of Notre Dame and a PhD from the University of Nebraska.

*God Knows Best About Joy* is the first book in the Fun Nun's® series, *God Knows Best About....* Each book will highlight Scripture passages that correspond with its theme. If you want more details about her forthcoming books, please contact her.

The Order of the Fun Nuns (OFN), which she founded has thousands of members. Members are encouraged to spread some joy each day in their own way. There is a membership card for you on the next page.

The Fun Nun® will make you laugh while you are learning! She speaks on topics related to humor, stress and self-image. If you need to add some life and zest to your program, invite The Fun Nun® to your next meeting! Contact her by any of the following ways:

| | |
|---|---|
| Phone: | 402-399-2474  Fax: 402-399-2686 |
| Email: | funnun@csm.edu |
| Web Site: | http://www.speakers-podium.com/funnun |
| Address: | College of Saint Mary |
| | 1901 S. 72nd St. |
| | Omaha, NE USA 68124-2377 |

**MEMBERSHIP CARD**

# ORDER OF THE FUN NUNS (OFN)
### OPEN TO ALL

*A MERRY HEART DOES LIKE GOOD MEDICINE*
PROVERBS 17:22

I, _____,
SPREAD SOME JOY EACH DAY
IN MY OWN WAY.

THE FUN NUN®
SISTER M. CHRISTELLE MACALUSO, RSM, OFN, PhD
COLLEGE OF SAINT MARY, 1901 S. 72ND ST., OMAHA, NE 68124-2377
402-399-2474, FAX: 402-399-2686, EMAIL: funnun@csm.edu
WEB SITE: http://www.speakers-podium.com/funnun

# Introduction

Books similar to this have taken quotes of famous persons or wise sayings and matched them with Bible verses. My book, *God Knows Best About Joy*, differs from these. I've taken the Bible theme of Joy, selected passages that represent this theme, and offered a personal reflection on them.

This is the first book of an intended series. I deliberately chose the theme of Joy to begin the series. As the Fun Nun® (hence, OFN, Order of the Fun Nuns) I speak often about the importance of joy in our lives. A banner in my office reads "Joy is the infallible sign of God."

There are many passages in the Bible that refer to joy, happiness, merriment and laughter. I have chosen to reflect on some of these in a way that I hope combines wit with wisdom.

*I chose The Living Bible because the translation uses words and expression that agree with common parlance.*

*My prayer is that you may grow in the joy of the Lord as you ponder the words in this book.*

The Fun Nun®
Sister Mary Christelle Macaluso, RSM, OFN, PhD
College of Saint Mary, Omaha, Nebraska USA

# GOD KNOWS BEST ABOUT JOY

THE FUN NUN®

SISTER MARY CHRISTELLE MACALUSO, RSM, OFN, PhD

*...he will make me smile
again for he is my God!*
Psalm 43:5

*God Knows Best About Joy*

There is so much in creation
to bring on a smile —
the grin of a baby,
a beautiful sunset, colorful flowers.
A smile is a special gift
God has given you.

Use it often.

Fun Nun®

*Always be joyful.  Always keep on praying.  No matter what happens, always be thankful for this is God's will for you who belong to Christ Jesus.*

1 Thessalonians 5:16-18

*God Knows Best About Joy*

**Prayer is the lifting up of your heart to God in adoration, thanksgiving, repentance and petition.
Prayer is communicating with God as you would a friend.**

**Trust your friend.
He is the source of all joy.**

Fun Nun®

*For it is silly to be*
*laughing all the time,*
*what good does it do?*

Ecclesiastes 2:2

# Laughing all day would be physically exhausting, but joy in the heart is energizing!

Fun Nun®

*Pray for the happiness
of those who curse you...*
Luke 6:28

*God Knows Best About Joy*

**Forgiving another
when you have been wronged
is to replace hate with love.
The Lord calls you to this.
Forgiveness comes
with a divine guarantee.
You will be filled with
a deep inner joy.**

Fun Nun®

*So I saw that there is nothing better for men than they should be happy in their work for that is what they are here for, and no one can bring them back to life to enjoy what will be in the future, so let them enjoy it now.*

Ecclesiastes 3:22

*God Knows Best About Joy*

**So much of life is lost
looking to the future or
brooding about the past while letting
the present moment slip by.**

**LIVE IN THE NOW
FOR A HAPPIER TOMORROW!**

Fun Nun®

*..."Zacchaeus!" he said, "Quick! Come down! For I am going to be a guest in your home today." Zacchaeus hurriedly climbed down and took Jesus to his house in great excitement and joy.*

Luke 19:5-6

*God Knows Best About Joy*

**Don't ever forget that
you are God's house (temple).**

**Pray and work to always
have your house in order.**

Fun Nun®

*There is a right time for everything.*
*A time to cry; a time to laugh...*

Ecclesiastes 3:1,4

*God Knows Best About Joy*

# Rejoice
# in your humanness and
# your ability to
# laugh!

Fun Nun®

## *Is there any such thing as Christians cheering each other up?...*

Philippians 2:1

**You need to support
and help others.
If you have made another
person on this earth smile,
your life has been
worthwhile.**

Fun Nun®

17

# Give your parents joy!
## Proverbs 23:25

*God Knows Best About Joy*

**Parents, here's a divine line that merits posting on the family refrigerator.**

*Children, adolescents, teenagers: READ THIS!*
**Place it deep in your hearts and live by it.**

Fun Nun®

*...He will rejoice over you in great gladness; he will love you and not accuse you. Is that a joyous choir I hear? No, it is the Lord himself exulting over you in a happy song.*

Zephaniah 3:17-18

*God Knows Best About Joy*

*God Knows Best About Joy*

# Doesn't that give you glory bumps?

# The love of God for you is infinite.

Fun Nun®

21

*...Rejoice before the Lord your God*
*in everything you do.*

Deuteronomy 12:18

*God Knows Best About Joy*

# Do you think that includes studying for finals, mowing the grass, cleaning, waiting for traffic, or struggling with the computer?

Fun Nun®

*But God in heaven merely laughs!*
*He is amused by all their puny plans.*

Psalm 2:4

**God has a sense of humor and
He gave one to you.
A sense of humor is the ability
to bring happiness
to the life of another person,
as well as your own.**

Fun Nun®

*Happy is the man who doesn't give in and do wrong when he is tempted, for afterwards he will get as his reward the crown of life that God has promised those who love him.*

James 1:12

**Remember, the Divine author doesn't
mean the temptation
to eat a piece of pie,
cake, candy or chips when you are trying
to lose weight!
Every time you overcome the temptation
to break a commandment,
your crown glows brighter and your
heart rejoices.**

Fun Nun®

28

*The good man
can look forward to happiness,
while the wicked
can only expect wrath.*

Proverbs 11:23

*God Knows Best About Joy*

# Your happiness comes from following the Lord's path. However, if you slip remember He is always ready to forgive.

Fun Nun®

*When you are reviled and persecuted and lied about because you are my followers — wonderful!*
*Be happy about it! Be very glad!*
*For a tremendous reward awaits you up in heaven...*

Matthew 5:11

*God Knows Best About Joy*

# Jesus said it.
# Believe it!
# You can meet adversity
# with God's help.

## Praise the Lord!

Fun Nun®

*...Joy rises in my heart*
*until I burst out*
*in songs of praise to him.*

Psalm 28:7

*God Knows Best About Joy*

**Praise God!
This holds true
even if you can't
hold a note!
The Lord listens to
the love of the heart,
and not just the sound waves.**

Fun Nun®

*For, after all, the important thing
for us as Christians
is not what we eat or drink but
stirring up
goodness and peace and joy
from the Holy Spirit.*

Romans 14:17

*God Knows Best About Joy*

**Food and drink can be
very pleasurable
but only
*goodness, peace,* and *joy*
satisfy the soul.**

Fun Nun®

*...The foolishness of thinking that wealth brings happiness.*

Ecclesiastes 5:10

# Do you get it?
# If you're happy, you're wealthy!
# Happiness doesn't need
# a bank account.

Fun Nun®

*...I bring you the most joyful news
ever announced, and it is for everyone!
The Savior
—yes, the Messiah, the Lord—
has been born tonight in Bethlehem!*

Luke 2:10-11

*God Knows Best About Joy*

Time is marked
by the birth of Christ in a stable.
A.D. means anno domino,
the year of the Lord.
Can you comprehend such love—
the creator of the world becoming
one of us?
Alleluia!

Fun Nun®

*I am radiant with joy*
*because of your mercy,*
*for you have listened to my troubles*
*and have seen the crisis in my soul.*

Psalm 31:7

**God always is willing
to embrace you in His love.
He is ready to hear your problems.**

**There is no limit
to God's love for you.**

Fun Nun®

42

*With good men in authority,*
*the people rejoice,*
*but with the wicked in power,*
*they groan.*

Proverbs 29:2

*God Knows Best About Joy*

# Have you heard anyone rejoicing?
## Republicans!
## Democrats!
## Independents!
## Are you listening?

Fun Nun®

# *A worthy wife is her husband's joy and crown...*

## Proverbs 12:4

**A worthy husband is
a wife's joy and crown!
If you're married,
and look at your spouse this way
YOU'RE DOUBLY BLESSED!**

Fun Nun®

*...The star appeared to them again, standing over Bethlehem. Their joy knew no bounds!*

Matthew 2:9-10

*God Knows Best About Joy*

**The wise men traveled
far to find Jesus.
You only need to look within
because you are His temple.
When was the last time
you paused to reflect
on your sacredness?**

Fun Nun®

*This is the day the Lord has made.*
*We will rejoice and be glad in it.*

Psalm 118:24

*God Knows Best About Joy*

**A-n-o-t-h-e-r day...**
**Do you rejoice or**
**do you groan?**
**Celebrate life!**
**Greet each day**
**with joy in your heart!**

Fun Nun®

*Then Jesus led them out along the road to Bethany, and lifting his hands to heaven, he blessed them, and then began rising into the sky, and went on to heaven. They worshipped him, and returned to Jerusalem filled with mighty joy...*

Luke 24:50-52

*God Knows Best About Joy*

**By His death and resurrection,
Jesus opened up heaven for you.
You can accept Him or reject Him.
The choice is yours.
May heaven be your lasting home
where you will be filled with
eternal joy
in the presence of God.**

Fun Nun®

51

*Hope deferred makes the heart sick,
but when dreams come true at last,
there is life and joy.*

Proverbs 13:12

**Dreams and hope come together.**
**When hope is weak,**
**dreams begin to fade.**
**If a dream is never realized,**
**is your faith strong enough**
**to accept that**
**God knows what is best for you?**

Fun Nun®

*But though I appreciate your gifts,
what makes me happiest is the
well-earned reward you will have
because of your kindness.*

Philippians 4:17

**Acts of kindness are priceless.
Whether in word or deed,
given or received,
these acts are rarely forgotten.
These are treasures
others — and you — need.**

Fun Nun®

*"Why are you angry?" the Lord asked him [Cain].*
*"Why is your face so dark with rage?*
*It can be bright with joy*
*if you will do what you should! ..."*

Genesis 4:6-7

**Remember that Cain killed Abel.
Hate, envy, jealousy,
violence, and rage
are destructive.
Only when you follow
God's commandments
will you have joy.**

Fun Nun®

*The women ran from the tomb,*
*badly frightened, but also*
*filled with joy,*
*and rushed to find the disciples to*
*give them the angel's message.*

Matthew 28:8

*God Knows Best About Joy*

When a dream comes true
sometimes fright does
dwell with joy.
You get the new job you wanted,
yet you are apprehensive
whether you can do what is expected.
Sharing your feelings
with the right people can help.

Fun Nun®

59

# *It is pleasant to see plans develop...*
## Proverbs 13:19

*God Knows Best About Joy*

**Planning helps develop
your creativity and resourcefulness.
Following through and
completing a project
gives satisfaction.
It adds something positive
to your life.
Are you reaching your goals?**

Fun Nun®

*When I pray for you,
my heart is full of joy.*

Philippians 1:4

*God Knows Best About Joy*

**God wants you
to pray for others.
All of us need prayers.
You're praying for
your brothers and sisters.
After all, don't you say,
"Our Father, who art in heaven?"**

Fun Nun®

*...Sarah shall bear you a son;
and you are to name him Isaac
("Laughter")...*

Genesis 17:19

*God Knows Best About Joy*

**Sarah was a very old women when she received this news.**

**In God all things are possible!**

Fun Nun®

*Your eyes light up your inward being.*
*A pure eye lets sunshine into your*
*soul....If you are filled with light*
*within, with no dark corners, then*
*your face will be radiant too,*
*as though a floodlight*
*is beamed upon you.*

Luke 11:34,35

*God Knows Best About Joy*

**May your face
always radiate with
the joy of the Lord.**

**How do you do this?
By walking with God and
living His word.**

Fun Nun®

*...All who seek for God shall live in joy.*

Psalm 69:32

*God Knows Best About Joy*

**If God is not an important part
of your life,
will all those things
you're are running after
bring you happiness?**

**Life on earth is but an instant
compared to eternity.**

Fun Nun®

*Then he took her by the hand and called, "Get up, little girl!"*
*And at that moment her life returned and she jumped up!*
*"Give her something to eat!" he said.*
*Her parents*
*were overcome with happiness...*

Luke 8:54-56

*God Knows Best About Joy*

**The love of parents for their child
is a reflection of
God's love for you.
You are to call God "Father."
God wants you to love Him with
your whole heart, soul and strength.**

Fun Nun®

*So cheer up!*
*Take courage*
*if you are depending on the Lord.*
Psalm 31:24

*God Knows Best About Joy*

# May there be no ifs, ands, or buts about your dependence on the Lord.

Fun Nun®

*...we Christians are God's house
—he lives in us—
if we keep up our courage
firm to the end,
and our joy and our trust in the Lord.*

Hebrews 3:6

**If your house five star quality?**
**Is it sturdy with faith;**
**clean with purity;**
**airy with hope;**
**insured with trust**
**and entertained with joy?**

Fun Nun®

*Play joyous melodies of praise
upon the lyre and on the harp.*

Psalm 33:2

*God Knows Best About Joy*

**Maybe you play
the piano or guitar.
When you use your musical talents
to praise the Lord,
remember it is the mood (joy)
not the medium
that gives Him praise.**

Fun Nun®

*It will be the same joy as that of a*
*woman in labor*
*when her child is born*
*— her anguish gives place to rapturous*
*joy and the pain is forgotten.*
*You have sorrow now, but I will see you*
*again, and then you will rejoice, and no*
*one can rob you of that joy.*

John 16:21-22

*God Knows Best About Joy*

How sorrowful good-byes;
how joyous the reunions!
Just think of it—
your greatest reunion
is still to come!

Fun Nun®

*The man who knows right from wrong and has good judgment and common sense is happier than the man who is immensely rich...*

Proverbs 3:13-14

*God Knows Best About Joy*

# *CHARACTER DEFINITELY COUNTS!*

Fun Nun®

*After greeting them,*
*he showed them his hands and side.*
*How wonderful was their joy*
*as they saw their Lord!*

John 20:20

# Christ said he would rise again, AND HE DID! He pulled a great joke on the devil!

Fun Nun®

*As his father was making final arrangements for the marriage, Samson threw a party for thirty young men of the village, as was the custom of the day.*

Judges 14:10-11

*God Knows Best About Joy*

# And you probably thought stag parties were the invention of modern society!

Fun Nun®

# *A fool's fun is being bad,*
# *a wise man's fun is being wise!*

Proverbs 10:23

*God Knows Best About Joy*

**So much evil is done in the name of "just having fun."**

**May all your fun
be a delight in God's sight.**

Fun Nun®

*If you want a happy, good life,*
*keep control of your tongue,*
*and guard your lips from telling lies.*

1 Peter 3:10

**Is that a big order for you?
The power of the undisciplined
tongue is mind-boggling.
For a happier life,
control your tongue.
Use it to stand up for what is right,
lift others up, and bring them joy.**

Fun Nun®

*But make everyone rejoice who puts
his trust in you.
Keep them shouting for joy because
you are defending them.
Fill all who love you
with your happiness.*

Psalm 5:11

*God Knows Best About Joy*

**Can others put their trust in you,
or are they fearful of you?
Have you stood up
for the rights of others,
or are you indifferent?
Have you filled those
who love you
with happiness or sorrow?**

Fun Nun®

*Deceit fills hearts
that are plotting evil;
joy fills hearts
that are planning for good!*

Proverbs 12:20

How is your heart
feeling these days?
Told anyone your plans lately?
They must be good plans.
If anyone would ask you,
"How do you plan to do good
for others?"
What would be your answer?

Fun Nun®

*...Ask, using my name,
and you will receive,
and your cup of joy
will overflow.*

John 16:24

Why is a "No" to a prayer,
not considered an answer?
You may feel sadness instead of joy.
God listens to your prayers
asked in Christ's name.
God's ways are not
always your ways, but
He knows what is best for you.

Fun Nun®

95

*What happiness for those*
*whose guilt has been forgiven!*
*What joys*
*when sins are covered over!...*

Psalm 32:1

*God Knows Best About Joy*

**TODAY you should thank God for
forgiving your sins and
filling your heart
with joy.
TODAY you also need to
forgive yourself.
Both are needed
for joy to enter your heart.**

Fun Nun®

97

*Though a man lives
a thousand years twice over, but
doesn't find contentment—
well, what's the use?*

Ecclesiastes 6:6

*God Knows Best About Joy*

**Celebrate life — don't begrudge it!
Contentment is built up by one
positive choice at a time.
Choose wisely.**

Fun Nun®

*Sarah declared,*
*"God has brought me laughter!*
*All who hear about this shall rejoice*
*with me. For who would have ever*
*dreamed that I would have a baby?*
*Yet, I have given Abraham*
*a child in his old age!"*

Genesis 21:6-7

*God Knows Best About Joy*

**Sarah was an old lady!
The power of God
knows no bounds.**

**Now that should make you
VERY HAPPY.**

Fun Nun®

*So be truly glad!*
*There is wonderful joy ahead,*
*even though the going is rough*
*for a while down here.*

1 Peter 1:6

*God Knows Best About Joy*

**Remember life is short;
live for heavenly joys.
When you get to heaven
there will be
no more stress
and downsizing!**

Fun Nun®

103

104

*...The dawn and sunset
shout for joy!*
Psalm 65:8

*God Knows Best About Joy*

# The psalmist is telling you to imitate nature — join its AM and PM shouts of joy and praise.

## Try it!

Fun Nun®

*A happy face
means a glad heart;
a sad face
means a breaking heart.*

Proverbs 15:13

*God Knows Best About Joy*

And a puckered face means
you ate a dill pickle!
Since the mind affects the body
and the body affects the mind,
you can become a happier person
by putting on a smile.
Pass that smile on to others.

Fun Nun®

*...Here on earth
you will have many trials and sorrow,
but cheer up,
for I have overcome the world.*

John 16:33

*God Knows Best About Joy*

**The Lord understands
the heaviness of your heart,
but He promises you
peace and joy
if you believe in Him.**

Fun Nun®

*Time went by and the child (Isaac)
grew and was weaned,
and Abraham gave a party to
celebrate the happy occasion.*

Genesis 21:8

**You need to celebrate
milestones in your life.
Have you looked
for opportunities to celebrate?
For example, learning some new
computer software,
exercising five days in a row,
finishing the pile of work on your desk....**

Fun Nun®

*Then I decided to spend my time having fun, because I felt that there was nothing better in all the earth than a man should eat, drink and be merry, with the hope that this happiness would stick with him in all the hard work which God gives to mankind everywhere.*

Ecclesiastes 8:15

*God Knows Best About Joy*

**Your life can't be
all work or all play.
Getting balance
(that doesn't mean 50/50!)
is the trick.
Keeping it balanced
will bring you joy.**

Fun Nun®

113

*...Let your lives overflow with joy and thanksgiving for all he has done.*

Colossians 2:7

*God Knows Best About Joy*

**Do you pause at the end of your day
to count your blessings?
Maybe your car started at 20 (below zero),
a long lost friend called,
you completed your "to do" list,
or someone made you laugh.
Thank God for all blessings —
large and small.**

Fun Nun®

115

*But may the godly man exult.*
*May he rejoice and be merry.*

Psalm 68:3

*God Knows Best About Joy*

# Are you a godly man or woman?
## If so,
## get ready to make merry!
Fun Nun®

*...Tell Aaron and his sons that they are to give this special blessing to the people of Israel: "May the Lord bless and protect you; may the Lord's face radiate with joy because of you; may he be gracious to you; show you his favor, and give you his peace."*

Numbers 6:22-26

*God Knows Best About Joy*

**Do you ask God to bless
your food before you eat?
Have you asked God for a safe trip?
Have you ever said, "God bless you"
to someone who sneezed?
Ask for God's blessings each day.
Nothing is too small for a blessing.**

Fun Nun®

*Happy are the kind and merciful,
for they shall be shown mercy.*

Matthew 5:7

*God Knows Best About Joy*

Did you ever step aside
from your pain
to say to another, "I forgive you."
If you cannot forgive, why not?
The Lord has shown you mercy.
Should you not do the same?
Don't rot in your resentment,
but rejoice in being merciful and kind.

Fun Nun®

121

*When a man is gloomy,*
*everything seems to go wrong;*
*when he is cheerful,*
*everything seems right!*

Proverbs 15:15

*God Knows Best About Joy*

**You are in control of your attitude.
You may not be able to change
some events in your life,
but you can change
your reaction to them.
The next time you drop
something on the floor,
thank God for the opportunity
to exercise!**

Fun Nun®

123

*...The whole earth has seen God's*
*salvation of his people.*
*That is why the earth breaks out in*
*praise to God,*
*and sings for utter joy!*

Psalm 98:3-4

*God Knows Best About Joy*

# Come join the choir!
## Practice times:
## MONDAY THROUGH SUNDAY
## 12 AM - 11:59 PM.

Fun Nun®

*Pleasant sights and good reports give happiness and health.*

Proverbs 15:30

*God Knows Best About Joy*

**You choose what you read
and what you watch.
Remember garbage in
is garbage out.
Feed your soul
healthy material.**

Fun Nun®

*Then Zilpah produced a second  son,
and Leah named him Asher
(meaning "Happy") for she said,
"What joy is mine!
The other women will think me
blessed indeed!"*

Genesis 30:12-13

*God Knows Best About Joy*

# You probably thought
# the only person
# with the name "Happy"
# was one of the seven dwarfs!

Fun Nun®

130

*Always be full of joy in the Lord;
I say it again rejoice!*

Philippians 4:4

*God Knows Best About Joy*

# This message is so important the apostle Paul felt he had to say it twice!

Fun Nun®

*Happiness comes to those
who are fair to others
and are always just and good.*

Psalm 106:3

The unjust can
never truly be happy.
Be fair, just and good.
Your spirit will be
bathed in joy.

Fun Nun®

*...Happy the man
who puts his trust in God.*

Proverbs 16:20

*God Knows Best About Joy*

**When Saint Peter lost his trust in Jesus as he walked on the water, he began to sink.**

**When you feel you are ready to sink with the burdens in your life, reach up to the Lord, and He will save you.**

Fun Nun®

135

*The news soon reached Pharaoh
"Joseph's brothers have come," and
Pharaoh was very happy to hear it,
as were his officials.*

Genesis 45:16

*God Knows Best About Joy*

# Do you rejoice
# at another's good fortune?

## If not,
## why not?

Fun Nun®

*A cheerful heart does good
like medicine,
but a broken spirit makes one sick.*

Proverbs 17:22

*God Knows Best About Joy*

**Years back someone said
cod liver oil
was the cure all!**

**Cheerfulness is
more palliative and with
no unpleasant aftertaste!**

Fun Nun®

*Only the person involved
can know his own bitterness or joy—
no one else can really share it.*

Proverbs 14:10

*God Knows Best About Joy*

**You are so unique
that no one can really experience
your sorrows and joys.
In times of trial and sorrow,
try to understand
when others support you
out of love and concern.**

Fun Nun®

*May the Lord continually bless you
with heaven's blessings
as well as with human joys.*

Psalm 128:5

*God Knows Best About Joy*

# Pass this blessing on
# and make someone else's day.

## Maybe you'll even start
## a chain reaction!

Fun Nun®

*...cheerful givers
are the ones God prizes.*

2 Corinthians 9:7

*God Knows Best About Joy*

For some, receiving is wonderful,
but giving is a chore.
Give with a smile on your face
and joy in your heart!
The size of the gift doesn't matter,
but the thought behind it does.
Sometimes the greatest gift
is your time.
Be one of God's prizes.

Fun Nun®

*Your words are what sustain me;*
*they are food to my hungry soul.*
*They bring joy to my sorrowing heart*
*and delight me...*

Jeremiah 15:16

# When was the last time you read the Bible?

## Its words are food for your soul and joy for your heart.

Fun Nun®

*...Why be discouraged and sad?*
*Hope in God!*

Psalm 42:5

*God Knows Best About Joy*

Would the hope in your heart
fill a thimble or
a swimming pool?

Remember...
little hope reflects little trust in the Lord.
The greater the hope
the happier you'll be.

Fun Nun®

*Reverence for God gives life,
happiness and protection from harm.*

Proverbs 19:23

**What does reverence mean?
Reverence happens when
deep respect and honor
mingle with awe and love.**

**Reverencing God opens you
to His love and protection.**

Fun Nun®

*Happy is the generous man,
the one who feeds the poor.*

Proverbs 22:9

*God Knows Best About Joy*

**Heed this, all scrooges of this world!
Remember, God uses your hands
to do his work.**

**What an honor
to be His representative at large!**

Fun Nun®

*Heart, body and soul
are filled with joy.*

Psalm 16:9

*God Knows Best About Joy*

## To be filled
## you have to rid yourself of
## what is displeasing to God.

## Follow His commandments
## and joy will enter.

Fun Nun®

*It is a wonderful thing to be alive!  If a person lives to be very old, let him rejoice in every day of life, but let him also remember that eternity is far longer, and everything down here is futile in comparison.*

Ecclesiastes 11:7-8

*God Knows Best About Joy*

# May you grow old gracefully because you do so joyfully.

## Life is too short to spend it being grouchy!

Fun Nun®

*Happy are those who long to be
just and good,
for they shall be
completely satisfied.*

Matthew 5:6

*God Knows Best About Joy*

_God Knows Best About Joy_

**If you long to be just and good
rather than rich and famous,
look at what God has
in store for you!**

Fun Nun®

*The time will come when God's redeemed will all come home again. They shall come with singing to Jerusalem, filled with joy and everlasting gladness; sorrow and mourning will all disappear.*

Isaiah 51:11

**Someday sorrow and mourning will disappear.
Every tear will be wiped away.
Gladness will be yours.**

**You have been redeemed,
but have you accepted
your redemption?**

Fun Nun®

*There will be great joy
for those who are
ready and waiting
for his return...*

Luke 12:37

*God Knows Best About Joy*

# ARE YOU READY?
# IF SO,
# ALLELUIA!
Fun Nun®

# BIBLE VERSES USED

## OLD TESTAMENT

| | |
|---|---|
| Proverbs | 3:13-14, 10:23, 11:23,12:4, 12:20,13:12,13:19,14:10, 15:13, 15:15, 15:30, 16:20, 17:22, 19:23, 22:9, 23:25, 29:2 |
| Psalms | 2:4, 5:11, 16:9, 28:7, 31:7, 31:24, 32:1, 33:2, 42:5, 43:5, 65:8, 68:3, 69:32, 98:3-4, 106:3, 118:24, 128:5 |
| Genesis | 4:6-7, 17:19, 21:6-7, 21:8, 30:12-13, 45:16 |
| Ecclesiastes | 2:2, 3:1,4; 3:22, 5:10, 6:6, 8:15, 11:7-8 |
| Numbers | 6:22-26 |
| Judges | 14:10-11 |
| Isaiah | 51:11 |
| Deuteronomy | 12:18 |
| Jeremiah | 15:16 |
| Zephaniah | 3:17-18 |

*God Knows Best About Joy*

# BIBLE VERSES USED

## NEW TESTAMENT

| | |
|---|---|
| Matthew | 2:9-10, 5:6, 5:7, 5:11, 28:8 |
| Luke | 2:10-11, 6:28, 8:54-56;11:34,36; 12:37, 19:5-6, 24:50-52 |
| John | 16:21-22, 16:24, 16:33, 20:20 |
| Philippians | 1:4, 2:1, 4:4, 4:17 |
| 1 Peter | 1: 6, 3:10 |
| Romans | 14:17 |
| James | 1:12 |
| 1 Thessalonians | 5:16-18 |
| Hebrews | 3:6 |
| Colossians | 2:7 |
| 2 Corinthians | 9:7 |

166

S. Joan Frances Gieie, SSND

*God Knows Best About Joy*

## BOOK ORDER FORM

Cost per copy of *God Knows Best About Joy*       $9.95
Postage and Handling per book                    $2.00

Send check or money order (in USA currency) made payable to **Sisters of Mercy**. Mail with form to: Fun Nun Books, College of Saint Mary, 1901 S. 72nd St., Omaha, NE USA 68124-2377.

Your Name: _____

Company: _____

Address: _____

City: _____ State: _____

Country: _____ Zip: _____

Telephone: _____ Fax: _____

Email: _____

$11.95 X_____Book(s) = Total: _____

## THANK YOU FOR YOUR ORDER!

168

*God Knows Best About Joy*

## CASSETTE TAPE ORDER FORM

Cost per tape including postage    $9.00

\_\_\_\_\_ Laughter/Jokes/Laughter

\_\_\_\_\_ Wellness and Your Funny Bone

\_\_\_\_\_ The Merry Christian

\_\_\_\_\_ Self-image and Interpersonal Relationships

\_\_\_\_\_ Communication and Interpersonal Relationships

\_\_\_\_\_ Stress: What's It All About?

\_\_\_\_\_ Relaxation Techniques

\_\_\_\_\_ The Mind/Body Connection

$9.00 X_____ = Total_____

Send check or money order (in U.S. currency) made payable to: **Sisters of Mercy**.
Mail form with the information on page 170 to:  The Fun Nun, College of Saint Mary,
1901 S. 72 St., Omaha, NE USA, 68124-2377

## THANK YOU FOR YOUR ORDER!

## Please send the tapes indicated on page 169 to:

Your Name: _____

Company: _____

Address: _____

City: _____ State: _____

Country: _____ Zip: _____

Telephone: _____ Fax: _____

Email: _____

*God Knows Best About Joy*